For Your Soul

Lonie Fitz

BookLeaf Publishing

India | USA | UK

Presentation by *BookLeaf Publishing*

Web: www.bookleafpub.com

E-mail: info@bookleafpub.com

ISBN: 9789363308008

First edition 2024

To the beautiful soul within you,

This is for your soul's journey- through the valleys of doubt and the peaks of triumph. Your soul is an eternal flame, deserving of every bit of love, honor, and celebration.

With all my love and gratitude,

Lonie Fitz

ACKNOWLEDGEMENT

To my family and friends,
You are the stars in my night sky,
You dance around my world,
Bringing light to my darkest
hours.

In the Garden of Life,
You are the vibrant flowers,
You are the ink in my pen,
The spark in my creativity,
To those whose cheers have lifted
me so high,

Your trust has fueled my
deepest drives

PREFACE

"For Your Soul" Is a testament to the transformative power of faith and the journey towards self-discovery and love. This book was inspired by my trials and struggles with self-confidence, love, and peace and it is through finding God that I was able to find them. It is my sincere hope that through these words, you too may find the inspiration and strength to overcome your struggles.

The inspiration for this book came during a profound period of my life when I was grappling with feelings of inadequacy searching for a deeper sense of purpose. I faced numerous obstacles that tested my faith and self-belief. It was during these moments that I turned to God, and in doing so, I discovered a wellspring of love and confidence that I wish to share with others.

"For Your Soul" is a collection of poems and reflections that delve into themes of faith, love, resilience, and self-discovery. Each piece is crafted with the intention of offering solace, encouragement, and a reminder of the divine strength that resides in each of us.

This book is structured to be a companion for your spiritual journey, a source of comfort and inspiration whenever you need it. Whether you are seeking motivation, a moment of peace, or simply a reminder of God's love, I hope these words resonate with you and offer the support you seek.

Self-Love

S- Seek within the quiet of your soul,
E- Embrace the light and you'll be whole.
L- Listen to your heart's Plea
F- Forgive your flaws, you'll be free

L- Love yourself with all your might,
O- Own your story, take delight.
V- Value every step you've walked
E- Embrace yourself, a gift God chalked

Mine

An eternal love, a love that gives birth,
It's only one like it on this Earth.

I stand in the mirror, and meet my gaze,
Embracing my flaws, in a gentle embrace.
For I am a masterpiece, unique and divine,
A creation of love, in this body of mine.

I trace the lines on my face, the stories they tell,
For they are reminders, of battles I've won,
They are reminders of times I thought I was
frail,
Proof of resilience, of all I have done.

I cherish my body, in all its glory,
For it has carried me through life's endless story.
I nourish it with kindness and tender care,
For it's the vessel that allows me to be here.

I celebrate my mind, a universe untamed,
A garden of thoughts, where dreams are framed
I feed it with knowledge and wisdom's embrace,
For it's the source of my strength, my saving
grace.

I honor my emotions, the highs and lows,
For they are the colors that make my world Go.
I allow myself to feel, without judgment,
without shame,
For it's through vulnerability, that self-love I
reclaim.

I forgive myself for the mistakes I have made,
For growth comes from lessons, in the choices
we've laid.
I release the past, with its burdens and weight,
Self-love blooms, when we learn to let go and
create.

I am deserving of love, in its purest form,
From myself, I am worthy, my heart does affirm.
Self-love is the foundation, on which I stand tall,
An unbreakable love, a love that conquers all.

Boundless Virtues

Faith removes limitations,
Love removes temptations
Hope ignites aspirations,
Strength calms our tribulations.

Joy brightens every day
Mindfulness helps us find our way
Wisdom guides our choices
Courage gives our hearts voices

Patience teaches us to wait
Kindness opens every gate
Gratitude brings contentment near,
Compassion wipes away every tear

Truth illuminates our path,
Justice balances the aftermath
Forgiveness frees us from the past,
Respect makes our bonds last

Perseverance pushes us through
Integrity keeps our actions true
Together these virtues make us whole,
These are the things that make us alive
These things will fill the void.

For Your Soul

For your soul,
Please meditate.
Make a journal of food you ate.
Laugh at the bad days,
Repent from your old ways.

For your soul,
Please do heal,
Search for things that seem real.
Embrace the day, cherish the night
Dance in darkness, find your light.

Walk in nature, breathe in deep,
Let the whispers of the forest seep.
Create with hands, heart, and mind,
You'll be surprised with what you find

Read the words that speak to you,
Let stories old and dreams anew,
Paint your world in colors so bright,
Lift your spirit, and take flight.

Kindness, sow in every land,
With each small gesture, lend a hand.
In giving, feel the joy begin,

A warmth that grows from deep within

Write your thoughts, your hopes, your fears,
Ink your journey through the years.
Reflect on food that fuels your days.
Honor your body in mindful ways.

In laughter, find a sweet release,
A moment's joy, a slice of peace.
Forgive yourself for past mistakes,
In repentance, a new path you'll take.

For your soul,
Please seek the calm,
Find in silence, a healing balm
In the simple, the pure, the true,
Discover the makings of you.

Dance in the rain, let the worries go,
Feel the earth beneath your toes.
Sing your heart out, loud and clear,
Let your voice dispel your fear.

Surround yourself with those who care,
Who lifts you up, who is always there.
Share your dreams, your joys, your pain,
In their love, find strength again.

Travel wide, explore the new,

In other cultures, perspectives brew.
See the world through different eyes,
Let wonder, like a phoenix, rise.

Practice patience, cultivate grace,
Move at your own pace
In every moment, find your song,
Know you are where you belong

Pray, if that's what guides your soul
or find a ritual that makes you whole
Connect with the divine, however, it speaks,
In sacred moments, solace seeks.

For your soul,
Please mediate,
Make a journal of the things you ate
Laugh at the bad days
Repent from your old ways

For your soul
Please meditate
Make a journal of the food you ate
Laugh at the bad days,
Repent from your old ways

For your soul,
Please do heal.
Search for things that seem real

For your soul
Find joy in play,
Let your inner child come out and stay.
Build and dream, and let go of the mold,
In your creativity, be bold.

Rest when you are weary, honor your need,
Let self-care be your creed.
In gentle moments, find your peace,
Let your worries and burdens cease.

In each sunrise, find a start,
A chance to fill and heal your heart.
In every sunset, let go with grace,
Embrace the night, a scared space.

For your soul,
Please meditate,
Make a journal of the food you ate
Laugh at the bad days,
Repent from your old ways

For your soul,
Please so heal,
Search for things that seem real

In this journey, be kind and true,
For your soul is a reflection of you

Nurture it, cherish it, let it shine,
In every heartbeat, the divine

Higher

Take me higher, beyond the sky,
Where dreams are born and eagles fly.
I Want to pass the limits set,
To reach heights I can't see yet.

Teach me to be more like you,
In all I say, in all I do.
Show me the path to find more
I want a heart so pure

If there's places that I fill empty
Fill me with your love so plenty
Pour wisdom into my soul.
Make me whole

Guide my steps through joy and sorrow
Give me hope for a better tomorrow
In moments I feel unsure
Grant me faith that's strong and pure
Help me see with clearer sight
To choose the good, to choose the right.

With every breath, with every beat,
In the people I meet,
Let your light shine through my eyes,

A light in the darkest skies.

Teach me patience. Teach me peace.
To find in danger, a release.
In every trial big or small,
Let me rise above all.

In your image, let me be,
A mirror of divinity.

Unique

God said I was uniquely and wonderfully made,
So I stand on that, I can do all things unafraid.
In his image, I find my worth,
A precious soul, since my birth.

 Satan said I wasn't anything,
So I disregard that, I know what I bring
In the lies, no truth I find
For God's love is always Kind.

In the mirror I see his grace,
Every feature, with every trace.
Crafted by the divine hand,
In his truth, I firmly stand.

No shadow of doubt can make me fall,
For I am cherished, loved by all
In the night- I am the light
Guided by faith, shining bright

My heart, a vessel of his love
A gift from the heavens above.
Through whispers of doubt may come my way,
In God's truth, I will always stay.

Every flaw, a testament to his art,
Every strength, a beat of His heart

So I walk with my head held up high
For I am seen through his eyes
Santan's words, they fade away,
In God's embrace, I find my way.

Uniquely made, wonderfully whole,
A beloved child, a cherished soul.
In His promises, I place my trust,
For in His image, I am just

Some Days

It's hard sometimes, I know
You'll have one foot in the door and the other
one out,
Some days you'll take five steps forward and
twenty steps back
But I promise you'll make it there.
One step at a time.
Keep praying, You'll be fine.
Your okay. You're where you belong.
No matter how long it takes.
God makes no mistakes.

Dreams

In the early morning, When the world is still,
A whisper calls, an emerging thrill
Deep within, where inhibitions play,
A flame is lit, Its here to stay

Purpose, elusive, like the morning mist,
A dream, a hope, that can't be dismissed.
It weaves through thoughts, twenty-four hours a
day,
An emerging calling that will not go away

In moments of doubt, when paths seem lost,
When dreams are weighed by heavy cost,
Purpose stands as a guide,
It gives us hope where doubt hides

Its found in laughter, in tears, in strife,
In every chapter of our life.
In the hands we hold, the hearts we touch,
In small, kind gestures that mean so much

Purpose isn't grand, or always clear,
It's in the love we give, the ones we cheer.
It's in the battles we fight,
In standing up for what is right

It's in the art we create
It's in the risk we take
In the whispers of the soul
In the things that make us feel whole.

With every step, with every breath,
Purpose guides us, beyond death.
It's the journey, not the end
That will allow your heart to mend

Don't try to find it in other lands,
But in the work of your own hands
In the dreams that set your heart on fire,
In the moments that lift you higher

For purpose lies in you, in me,
These choices that we make,
Our desire to live with meaning everyday

The Reason

I always wondered why
Growing up people would tell me one thing,
They would say "Love yourself"
I didn't understand what that could truly mean.

Once I found it. I can't let go,
Loving myself became my gold,
I only dreamed of a love so pure, a love to
behold.
There is nothing like my own embrace
I am a love that can't be replaced

In a world that seeks validation,
Loving yourself brings liberation.
For when you love yourself, you become the
key,
You've mastered acceptance and you are free

No longer bound by others expectations,
You embrace your flaws and imperfections
You learn to celebrate your unique essence,
And find beauty in your own presence.

Its a journey of self-discovery

A path that leads to inner harmony.
You learn to listen to your hearts desires,
And follow your dreams, igniting inner fires.

When you love yourself, you become whole,
No longer seeking validation from other souls
You realize that your worth is not defined
By the opinions of those who are blind.

You'll always feel at home
You'll never feel alone
If you honor yourself, you will find
That you are worthy and devine

Beyond the Boundaries of Thought

The thoughts in my head, I know they're not
real,
They don't define me, nor shape how I feel.
They only reveal where my boundaries lie,
But I am more, I reach beyond the sky.

I will not let these thoughts dictate,
Nor define my path, nor seal my fate.
They will not collaborate with my reality,
For in my heart, I hold my truest clarity.
There's more to me than fleeting words,
More than echoes that are often heard.
In every breath, in every choice,
I find my power, I find my voice.

I am more than what my mind projects,
A tapestry of dreams, hopes, and prospects.
In the silence, I find my truth,

With every step, I redefine,
The boundaries set, the limits entwined.
In my essence, pure, and free,
I am more than words, I am simply me.

Hope

Sometimes life gets too hard,
Decisions are difficult,
And dreams don't seem to far.
In times like these... remember who you are.

When the weight of the world
Feels to heavy to bear,
And the path ahead
Seems clocked in despair,
Take a moment to breathe and know,
Within you is something that will glow.

In the darkest nights,
When hope feels thin,
Remember the stregth
That resides within.
You are more than the trials you face,
A soul of courage, beyond grace.

Each choice may feel
Like a mountain steep,
And dreams might seem
Beyod your reach.
But deep inside, you hold a star,
A guide to remind you of who you are.

So when the road is tough,
And you falter or fall,
Remember your essence,
Stand tall, stand tall.
For in your heart,
There's a boundless spark,
Guiding you forward.
Even in the dark.

Sometimes life gets too hard,
Decisions are difficult,
And dreams don't seem to get far.
In times like these.... remember who you are.

Affirmation

I refused to be defined,
I am me. I claim all that's mine.
I embark on a journey, deep within my core,
To banish the darkness and restore

With courage as my guide.I face the abyss.
Confronting the demons that I cannot dismiss.
I shine a light on the darkest corners of my soul,
Unveiling the wounds that need to be made
whole.

I acknowledge the pain, the hurt, and the fear,
Releasing them with every tear.
I embrace forgiveness, for myself and others,
Letting go of grudges, freeing my spirit to
rediscover.

I seek healing in the the form of love,
Drawing strenghth from the god above.
I fill the void with self-compassion and care,
Nurturing my soul, mending what's been torn
and bare.

As the darkness receded, light begins to seep
filling the spaces that were once so deep.

I find solace in the beauty of my own
being,Embracing the flaws, the scars, the seeing.

For it is in the process of healing and growth,
That I find the strength to let go.

I release the dark places of my soul,
Allowing love and light to take control.
I am reborn, transformed, and set free
My soul is free

Forgive

Mistakes are always made,
Words are spoken in anger, making hearts fade
Forgiveness is not a weakness, nor a surrender
But a strength that transcends, a love so tender.
It's a choice to release the burdens we bear,
To let go of resentment and show that we care.

Its a gift we give ourselves

Children of God

Life is full of confusion,
Full of sin and delusion,
Sometimes it's hard to see the light,
Sometimes it's hard to fight

Paths diverge, choices unclear,
Hearts can get weighed down by fear.
In the maze of hopes and dreams,
Nothing is quite as it seems.

Yet in the choas, there's a mark,
A guide in the dark.
A chance for a higher call,
A promise that we're not alone at all.

As a child of God, we stand,
Guided by a loving hand
Through sin and mistakes,
Through the heartaches and heartaches,

There's a strength that lies within,
A resilience that begins.
Hope is found in every dawn,
In love we've built upon.

Through the trials, through the tears,
Faith can conquer all our fears.
In His embrace, we find our grace,
A calm in life's face pace

In our hearts, a truth will shine,
As children of the divine
Life is full of twists and turns
This is true...
But know this one thing through and through:
In the chaos, find your grace,
And walk this path with love's embrace.

Anxious?

Anxiety feels like...

A storm inside the sea,
Waves of worry crashing over me.
A weight that sits on my chest
A restless heart that cannot rest.

A whisper that grows into a scream
A working nightmare, a shattered dream.
An endless loop of what-is and fears,
A mind that drowns in uncried tears

A shadow lurking in the night
A constant battle between dark and light
A knot that tightens without end
A foe that masks itself as a friend

A heart that races without cause,
A moment's pause that never thaws
A feeling of being out of place,
A longing for a safe embrace.

An invisible chain, a silent cry,
A constant question: why, oh why?
A need for comfort, for release,

A desperate plea for inner peace.

Anxiety feels like this and more,
A storm that shakes you to your core.
But know in this fight, you're not alone,
For strength and courage can still be grown.

The Ugly Thing

Insecurity is a heavy chain around your heart
A suffocating grip that never lets go
It's the constant feeling of being exposed
Of every flaw and imperfection laid bare

Its the sting of every sideways glance
The echo of every harsh word spoken
A relentless barrage of self-doubt
That leaves you feeling small and broken

Insecurity is a storm raging inside
A whirlwind of fear and uncertainty
It's the tighteining of your chest, the trembling of
your hands
The feeling of being trapped in your own skin

It's the knot in your throat, the lump in your
chest
The never-ending battle with your own
reflection,
The constant comparison to an unattainable
standard
That leaves you on an endless quest for
validation

Always remember that you are not defined by insecurity. It's just a feeling. It's not who you are. You are worthy. You are enough.

Luke 11

Our Father in the sky
We lift our hearts and call to You.
Your name is holy, pure, and bright,
We know you are here day and night.

Let Your kingdom come our way,
Your will be done by us today.
On this earth, let love shine clear,
Just like in heaven, always near.

Give us the food we need each day,
For the strength we need every day
Forgive our wrongs, wipe them way
Make us more like you, we pray.

Keep us safe from tempting things,
Guide our steps on steady wings.
Protect us from what's dark and wrong,
With Your love, we stay strong.

For Yours is the kingdom, big and grand,
The power, like the ocean, and
The glory, like the morning sun,
In Your love, are one.

Amen.

Breath Work

I breathe in
Worries, thoughts, and depression,
I breathe out
Peace, love, and self-expression.

With each inhale, I draw in light
The shadows, the doubts, the hidden fright
I breathe in the chaos, the storm within,
The tangled webs where fears begin.

With each exhale I release the strain
The burdens are heavy, the silent pain.
I breathe out light in, for all it seems
Casting away the haunting dreams.

I breathe in
The weight of unshed tears,
I breathe out
Strength to face my fears.

In the stillness of this moment, I find
A space to quiet my restless mind.
I breathe in the noise, the clamor, the din,
Letting it swirl, then fade within.

I breathe out calm, a warm glow
A river of peace gins to flow
With each breath, a piece of me,
Find freedom, finds clarity.

I breathe in
The echoes of the past
I breathe out
The wisdom that healing takes.

Each breath a bridge from then to now,
A sacred vow
I breathe out
The wisdom that healing takes.

I breathe in lessons, the trials, the strife,
I breathe out renewal, my life

I breathe in
The fragments of a broken heart,
I breathe out
The courage to restart

I breathe in the world, in all its hues,
I breathe out the best of me, renewed.
I breathe in worries, thoughts, and depression,
I breathe out peace, love, success, and
progression.